Dolefully,
A Rampart Stands

My Love Is a Dead Arctic Explorer

In No One's Land

Dolefully,
A Rampart Stands

Paige Ackerson-Kiely

PENGUIN POETS

PENGUIN BOOKS

An imprint of Penguin Random House LLC
penguinrandomhouse.com

Copyright © 2019 by Paige Ackerson-Kiely
Penguin supports copyright. Copyright fuels creativity, encourages diverse voices, promotes
free speech, and creates a vibrant culture. Thank you for buying an authorized edition of this book
and for complying with copyright laws by not reproducing, scanning, or distributing any part of it
in any form without permission. You are supporting writers and allowing Penguin
to continue to publish books for every reader.

Acknowledgments to the original publishers of the poems in this book appear on page 79.

LIBRARY OF CONGRESS CATALOGING-IN-PUBLICATION DATA
Names: Ackerson-Kiely, Paige, 1975– author.
Title: Dolefully, a rampart stands / Paige Ackerson-Kiely.
Description: New York, New York : Penguin Books, [2019] | Series: Penguin poets
Identifiers: LCCN 2018031701 (print) | LCCN 2018032403 (ebook) |
ISBN 9780525504610 (E-book) | ISBN 9780143132684 (paperback)
Subjects: | BISAC: POETRY / American / General.
Classification: LCC PS3601.C56 (ebook) | LCC PS3601.C56 A6 2019 (print) |
DDC 811/.6—dc23
LC record available at https://lccn.loc.gov/2018031701

Printed in the United States of America
1   3   5   7   9   10   8   6   4   2

Set in Bembo MT Std
Designed by Ginger Legato

CONTENTS

Dolefully,
A Rampart Stands

Inventory of Ramparts

The pier shed its long
splinters into the lake.

A dinghy rubbed the side of the dock
but the dock was still.

Some kids ditched a canoe in the reeds
—the boy's voice was a reed—

they pulled it up the embankment by a rope
where no one could see it from water

or shore. His voice covered everything.
This isn't an opportunity to talk about the body,

how many dogs you get to have over
the course of a life. I'd reckon 6, if you take

good care of them. I'm going back in time
to hold the boy's head underwater.

Just to give him a little scare. The canoe
had vanished when they returned

and his voice became a basket
pushed down a river—nothing specific—

and anyway, this isn't an occasion to talk
about the body. I'm busy going, I need

to go, back through those boggy years to kiss
all of the dogs. Hard, on the mouth.

THE LESSON

He was wearing a light denim jacket. The north wind was a whisper, egging him on. The girl had a high, anxious laugh. She was supposed to be in class, taking a math test. None of this matters: they were in an alley that belonged to the dogs and the trash that gathered against the back fence. Beyond the fence was a road that eventually swept past the farmlands. His Grandfather lived in one of the old farmhouses the town turned into elderly apartments. Once, when camping, his Grandfather threw the snake he caught and intended to keep as a pet into the fire, where they later roasted hotdogs. He cried a little in the tent, but it was of no use. The girl was kicking pebbles, looking down. She startled when he grabbed her hand. He removed his jacket and she closed her eyes to a pasture dotted with buttercups. The lesson of enduring for the sake of someone else was one she had already mastered, so she thought of the little flowers and the snakes and bugs they fed and housed without pretension, and willed herself to blossom for the 5 minutes it would take. Before she snuck from school that day, the teacher went around the room asking each student what they wanted to be when they grew up. When her turn came she said quietly, no—resolutely: *A mother.* Everyone laughed but the teacher. The teacher seemed angry.

INHERITANCE

Deep-sixed for wont of something—
firm feelings, for example—or stacked china
pushed toward the back
of the cabinet. Not to be used, nor eaten
from. There are a dozen ways to give
to one's neighbor: The fence, cup of sugar,
removal of snow and what it portends.
You may have the air I sucked;
the gossip I told things to.
O hey there gorgeous, scaling the bannister
of the mortgage I shall inherit, meekly,
in some failing town: There is no winning
except to remember I am so lonesome—
the lenders call, they call and I answer,
and so they at least are fed, are full,
as the feral thing making early residence
there—giddy, rifling the dank closets
before anyone else can get in.

SHINE

My reputation when I stand beneath the stars
is one of tolerance.

It's dark out. No one can see me.

I make the shape of a woman standing
in a shed. How many of you can say the same?
Billions and billions served.

I want to impress the stars: carry
a bundle of sticks affixed to a strap
across my back. Walk 4 miles
or no miles at all.

At dawn, I will make a fire. No
biggie. Just another miracle
I may have had a part in.

The stars do not eat my breakfast.
A man eats my breakfast. Like the stars
he cannot take care of me very well.
But oh does he burn.

So I draw the water from the tap.

I draw the tap from memory.

Simple Story of Illumination

If you press a flashlight to your palm your hand will glow. All stories of illumination are basically the same. It was March, raining bitterly, and I was drunk. You came up behind me. Ear splitting bells rang and a bright light flashed in the North. After this I beheld, and lo, I couldn't count how many times I had waited to be touched in the rain, behind the barn, fingers of wet matches striking softly. No one could number the tall grass purring against my calves. I looked into a foggy distance: The farmer held an old bath towel with which he rubbed, one-by-one, his flock of lambs dry. I wondered how I might come to his aid, but thought instead to be left alone, wet and catching cold. Then I heard beasts and men alike, and all that is in them, singing. Who are these mad creatures we refuse to put down, and why was I so affrighted to abandon my mind and rise up in song? I walked home, drew a bath, then disappeared into the couch. Later, I followed you to the bedroom and undressed. Before me you made the shadow of a man and I was not afraid.

THE ROSE BUSH

Murder is also classical.
I know what you deserve.

Dieback all the way back
before you were born ugly
in the cradle, pretty at the table.

You put your hands over everything
the throats limned, the tags snipped—
your throat snipped, your hands bit
the roses nip and nod.

If you want to love a thing forever
don't take your eyes off its face.

The Cardinal

Late-winter, struggling snow off the porch, he paused to marvel at the leafless Norway maple couching a bird. The cardinal's gaze was protracted, hard against his face, made him feel as though he had trudged through a lightless forest and collided with a body hanging from a branch. He had no idea how long it had been there, in that tree, when he suddenly recalled reading of several crimes the past week, one involving a mob vs. a young woman. Under the bird's gaze he shrank to remember the dress had been torn off, her body left like Culp's Hill to reclaim its breastworks, a parapet of yellow tape cordoning off where she lay, where no one could cross to maybe get a little space and reflect, the knolls shrugging at the stupid question of him, standing right there. He said the names of his children. He said the time of day. The bird continued to stare. Stare of the young woman now contained in a bunting to be set ablaze, to return red to a body, to answer a question about leaving for good and taking your passion with you. Not even inspired to flight when his ex-wife's truck roared into the driveway, his bundled children climbing into the cab for more days than he cared to think about. Squawking. Squawking.

FOLDING CHAIRS

The folding chairs are separated while mating,
and lined up around the table for a different duty.

I splash my face with water from the chafing dish—
when has there not been an event requiring my sobriety?

The paper plate on top is covered in dust and discarded.
I'm 40 years old and I am just like everyone else

as Echo said whatever was said to her—
come forth, you among us who can discern a true apology.

Little blonde children cut each other's bangs
in the church bathroom.

For now it's all a big joke;
the ham blushes in strings from the carving station.

But the anger will surface once families get home,
kick off their boots in the mudroom. I am afraid

I will continue to burn the supper. I am afraid
I have not made enough for everyone.

S.

Worms unspool in shallow puddles

and are lifted as windsocks by the stick of a beak.

You call a friend to let something unsavory

slip from your mouth. She doesn't pick up.

Way out in the aspen grove, a treed cat

climbs higher still. The note read:

I AM SO SORRY. The s's make the path of a bowling ball,

knocked twice against the gutter guards, not

the straight metal spine of the ladder you drag

through the woods coaxing, *come down,*

come home to me.

LACONIA

I know what you're thinking right now. It's true she took the first job after high school. What can you do. Sometimes they come from a black scribble, words like couch, too many long-nippled hounds rushing the driveway. I know what it looks like to you. This is her peak. The bonfire by the lake. It's fall, everyone wears the same navy blue hoodie. I want to go on, but what's the point: She arrived with a man, slightly older. They screeched into the pull-off, dust like a smoke machine heralding their duet. He heaved the cooler from the truck bed. She touched her face nervously, linked her arm through his. I watched them walk the narrow path to the pit. Occasionally, this time of night, you hear loons calling across the water, the sound is foggy, sad, the way it fades toward the end, like a dinghy sighing before it turns to face a storm. But not quite yet. The wind picked up and he pulled her into him, unzipped his sweatshirt and wrapped it around her, too. There was nothing we could do. Sometimes they come from thirst, the way lips meet and separate, a last sip of flat soda shook onto the asphalt, bottle turned in for a nickel then crushed. You don't need me to tell you what happens next: 25 of them drinking and layering on twigs and brush. The night had become black like the space where a tooth used to be. Like the absence of tools. Chiseling the hard ground with your bare hands or maybe just kicking out a hole. You know what I mean. It's hard to think about a life before. He had an idea. Sometimes they come from a need to keep warm, or watch, in the face of a problem. Sometimes the problem is fixed, the way your organs stay inside your body even when you've lost everything else. It seemed like the fire had always been roaring. He grabbed a beer from the cooler, it felt like a flagpole in his hand, like it had rained and it was March. When was the last time he shimmied to the top of anything—couldn't remember—chucked the can whole into the blaze. You know the rest. Tell me what you heard. Did you hear the explosion. It started as a hiss, then burst with such force—sometimes they come from anger, sometimes ignorance, the end result is the same. The can unfurled under the pressure, the sharp blade of it into her eye, blood from her socket petaled her cheek. We could feel her breathing, beating, see her red eye, black hair plastered to her neck, and the pike dive, face first to the ground. The loons suddenly screaming: *where did you go? Tell me where I am!* The loons screaming and screaming, trying to locate a familiar, trying so goddamn hard to know something about love and a place before you go extinct.

Murmuration

They are not calling to you
from the top of the oak tree

or the wires stretched
from eaves to transformer

but they are speaking all the same—

as when you were a child
yelling your own name into a box fan

your voice chopped like the long
slender note of a carrot
in pieces on the floor

swept up by someone else,
someone who scolded
dirty things

should not touch the mouth—
as they threw them all away.

ALL AROUND THE MULBERRY BUSH

I don't want to know the future.

Ok, I do.

At first, you are strong. You turn the crank hard, smile knowingly at a friend because it can't go on this way forever. You turn. You bite your tongue, keep turning, your friend grows bored and leaves like autumn. At a certain point, it occurs to you that something isn't working. You shake the box, hold it to your ear. You can hear the parts inside clink like tiny gears come loose or a dozen baby teeth dropped into a glass jar, one-by-one. You resume turning, but slowly and for years, feeling for a stutter or catch. You are alone, it is the only penance a busy life allows. Your kids leave for college, for jail, for their own well-worn cranks. You keep turning, and eventually the whole damn box explodes. You scream. It's over. You tell your acquaintances about the exhilaration of surprise, even though you are a woman who can see it coming for a mile. You don't tell them about the pop, the pain in your arm, how when you close your eyes you see yourself being chased by your self. No, no. No one describes that part. The bushes knocked free of fruit and leaf, standing around naked, their thin limbs whipped by snow, by your turning, or beat upon by a sun hard and bright as a pop song playing them to death. You're standing still now, looking across the lawn like it's the end of a movie, and you think you should be crying but you've acted the part so badly it's hard to feel for you. No one can feel *for* you. You turn to the door—time to go inside. Pity is the rage of the lazy.

The Pine Tree

Sometimes the boughs sweep low
across the grass. This is called skirting.

Sometimes the boughs drop cones to the ground,
and walking barefoot beneath, you slice
your soft arch on the prickle, cry out.
This is called begetting.

Sometimes the boughs rust from the top
and the rust moves down, like working
a tight dress over your arms, your head.
This is called Pine Wilt.

When you put on the dress you get to die.
26.2% mentally ill in any given year.
Think of me naked in your backyard,
but not too long.

Working Stiff

All of the horses are broken.
All of the earth is turned.
You hear your name
on some wind but keep walking.
Your thoughts are a cot folded, propped
against the wall. There are so many waiting.
They are unwell. Let the fields cry a little
in the rain so no one sees.
Let it open up all over a man.
All over.

Adopting a New Currency

Our new currency made a celebratory entrance. She came in droves, heaps of riven brocade, steam trunks without the vapor rising up. We had misgivings, made our eyes into cattle lowering under a rainstorm while the grass smelled afraid, clumped and collected in our soles, could not be shook free. She ate through our rations; we touched the parts of her that swung. She ate through our rations; we kept all of our medicine in a small, white lockbox. I had the only copy of the key, practiced turning it in my closed fist, heard people coughing and tightened my fist until it couldn't be opened. The first time in my life I held something of value was a robin chick pushed early to flight and pummeled to ground, if you can say it that way. The slap of a wallet thrown to linoleum after an argument. Nursing is what one comes to after birth or war, but I was a boy at the time, fashioning paper cranes out of the worthless bills she replaced, lining them up in the shoebox as if being around some familiar form could soothe the bird back to health. It didn't work the way I saw it. You can spend your whole life caring for one single thing—you can grow it, pretend to see it everywhere. Our new currency was lighter than her forebearer, smaller too, and while we felt decent enough protecting her, I still tried my best to save the pills for the children that they might fly so far away.

WORK AS A MAN

All my work as a man
all my work as a man, my girl—

under a layer of paper ash
the burn cage two miles out.

Men who consume, men who routinely
touch off, my girl with folders

and notebooks. My girl in trousers meets
the desk, knee brushing under.

It's hard not to be turned on, all my
work and my girl in the office or

eating lunch from a brown paper bag
in the park we paid plenty for.

My girl under a layer of paper ash,
how she makes copies for other men

who alight, who char and scald,
bend over the machine: *I just can't*

get this to work. The front of her
trousers, where she wipes her fine hands—

all my work as a man, my girl,
please, let me do it for you.

CAPTIVITY

Inside a cage the dog snarls
and snaps, even the air is torn.
Inside the house the man's voice
is a bed turned over by cops.
They find nothing but their own anger,
some old tissues. They leave the place a mess.
You want to investigate silence.
It's Tuesday, the sun is a newly
opened can of mandarin slices,
though it's never hunger that wakes you.
You step outside, listen for a daffodil
pulling on its yellow slicker,
but cannot hear a thing. After a while,
you learn to feel for the rain.

Winter Moth

She never thought of the last thing he said to her, except on January 5th, when everyone in town put their Christmas trees out by the side of the road. Slender, upended, with silver tendrils that would pick up wind and wave, one tentacle to another, not so much a goodbye as a final, languorous stretch. She stood watching from the front step, in a fraying silk robe she received as a gift eight years ago. Back then, one might remark how it fluttered over her body. The breeze always befriends the beautiful; it is one way movies are like real-life. It was cold; the snow downy, difficult to pack, and the slightest gust caused it to skirt her bare ankles. Eventually, some guy stopped, hopped out of his rear loader, and threw the tree into the compactor. The smell of vomit and rotten meat from the maw of it. The compactor crushed the tree—the sound of those delicate limbs snapping, one by one, like he had something dark and classical against her. He said: *that's the end of that.* In the tumult, some needles were loosed from the branches and flew out onto the snow behind the truck. They looked like larvae of the Winter Moth, an early dispenser, active well into January under the right conditions. The female attracts a cloud of males. She isn't much to look at—small, nearly wingless, and still while they take turns. Please don't feel badly about where this is going. The difficult thing about joy is not the end of joy, but the preparation for the end of joy—noticing those looking on who do not feel it, noticing the pristine drift deliquescing to a muddy puddle, awaiting evaporation. The view of the back of his head as he drives off.

MEADOW REDACTION

You were given everything.
There is no other way to put it

without making a list: the table's sturdy legs,
annual phlox around the mailbox, meeting

a beautiful woman in a bar, the entire
month of June. I went to the farthest meadow

laced up by weed and bowed by the curve
of a highway. I settled into the saw grass,

the blood grass, the blue blue grass, the blades.
You could mow it high and tight. You could land

a helicopter dead in the center and bend
your cousin over the fence. Coat it with asphalt

and long yellow lines, park all of your cars close
and loving. I'm not challenging, just noticing.

It would be so easy to strangle, smother, rake it up,
scratch it loose. Post detour signs every four feet.

Lay your gravel path.
Dig out a pond, fill it with water!

The boat is a crescent of silver birch
I punch my body into. Sometimes, you let me sleep.

I am grateful for each morning.
Witness to doves worming the puddle,

witness to dew magnifying each leaf, the feeling
of unhooking a tight bra in a hot car

—you were given everything—

I put a handful of soil in my pocket, in my mouth,
the flowers, the petals coming out.

BALLAD OF LITTLE PREPARATION

The water was cold and fast.
I scolded the horses who would not follow
past the shallows, and cursed the wagon that tilted
and took on water, until all of my belongings—
matches, comb, tricorn hat, looking glass,
Nintendo 64, and also my gun—cannonballed deep.

One by one my possessions resurfaced,
glided toward the edge, bumped gently against rocks,
until the horses lowered their excuses for faces
and nuzzled the shore's growing cache.

But the gun never bubbled or surfaced or called,
though I waded through silt and plunged in once or twice,
as the night dropped its curtains with a long dusty thud,
and the stars burned like carrot-top kids at high noon.

All these days alone—I'd forgotten its use—
cattails gave me no trouble and there was a person
I loved. I imagined her smelling the top of my head.
I considered her ripping our dinner from earth
and scraping the eyes off potatoes.

I made a fire like you would a bed and tied the reins
to my good leg. How was I to know they were coming
for me? The horses broke free but stayed close.
The night ended when it was supposed to. I heard bells in the distance
and thought of Milosz. I never had talent for the moral.

LIBERATION POEM

I was riding my horse through the desert, when three young men cast their shadows of long knotted rope from the horizon line. In all my days I'd come to two conclusions: I should be a miller and grind the yellow stalks like stone to sand, or I should be a farmer and hum the seed up to the sky. I rode my horse through the desert, which is a way of saying there is no answer, for nothing of consequence grew, when three young men, the shadow of flagpoles mid-hoist, came near. I touched my face and it was my face. I gripped the mane and it was not a mane. It was canes of cholla sloughed of needle and flesh, full of oblong holes. The young men stood still the way a coyote menaces an old mare. The old mare! She neighs on and on. Fourteen hands at the withers and a dozen ancient words for grass, where she is finally taken down. I touched my arm and it was an arroyo. I touched the sagebrush and it was my boot touching the chest of one young man. I touched myself in the bathroom of the Best Western, police cars blaring the parking lot to obedience. I do not remember coming outside, the frying pan of asphalt, the quavering air. I closed my hand around the doorknob, pulled gently. I do not remember gently. The gum in my mouth, watermelon, grown in patches during monsoon—I do not remember anything so tender as those rotting globes swarmed by ants, leaking red, rind picked clean before harvest. I fell to my knees and no one tried to catch me. I fell to my knees and made love to what was there.

The Grandmothers

In spite of what one pictures,
there is no bustle, no bonnet,
no consideration for the teats
swollen like trousers thrown
over a ladder in a soaking rain—
bedewed heifer stock-still in a particular pasture.
There is no particular pasture,
only miles of New Hampshire duplexes.
No covered wagons or turrets,
only sedans on their way to church.
Once inside everyone shuts-up, or everyone came
already shut-up, it's hard to know the difference.
The songs, though, the songs are exactly the same.
There can be no longing for another history—
it's hymn-plain and stirred with a big wooden spoon.
But the beatings have moved.
The beatings are located in the basement or shed
when they used to be out on the prairie, reddening
the sky, little dust drops children ran their toes across.
Whose tears made these? The beatings don't say
in the dark. The beatings scuffed into the wall
of a newly remodeled home. For each one,
10 more hard miles of trail leading east—
no fires at the campsite, no advice from older women
who have been that way, no map.

Hole in the Wall

O crude ballast stumbled over en route to fiery drink! O limestone steps quarried from Canada and the cast iron jamb propping the bar's doorway! Inside you will sit, so thirsty, you don't have to wait for anyone specific. O course of adulthood stumbled half-dead into, and grasped with insectile tentativeness! Invariably they enter the bar in swarms, released by genital and propelled by genital, the beautiful lips of request, so deeply, so deeply buzzing it makes an exclamation mark curl. They say a breeding pair of termites look for a suitable home, bore a hole in the wall, seal themselves in, and commence mating. The bar is worn, is bearing down behind the shrubbery. From your stool you anticipate approach, drinking, she comes to you this way and that. The thing is, you might not know you have a problem until you knock on wood and it sounds hollow. By which point you are out of luck. She's found a way inside; she's eating away at the sturdiest parts. You can try setting yourself on fire. You can drink all the poison in the joint. Just understand: You are going to have to take them all with you when you go, even the ones you cannot bear to love back.

ADMINISTRATION

The hay gathered itself into neat rectangles.
The road longed for a spine and so came the passing lane.

I sat in my office, alone, at last, without exclamation.
There was the book I kept meaning to read.
There was the plant I kept meaning to water.

And so I learned my touch could not be heard.
Nothing called to me except for myself.

I peered into the hallway, for where else do the inconsolable roam?
I comforted the window, its view of the other window.

The glass bore prints of the quiet janitor.
Way up high I could see where the moths get out.

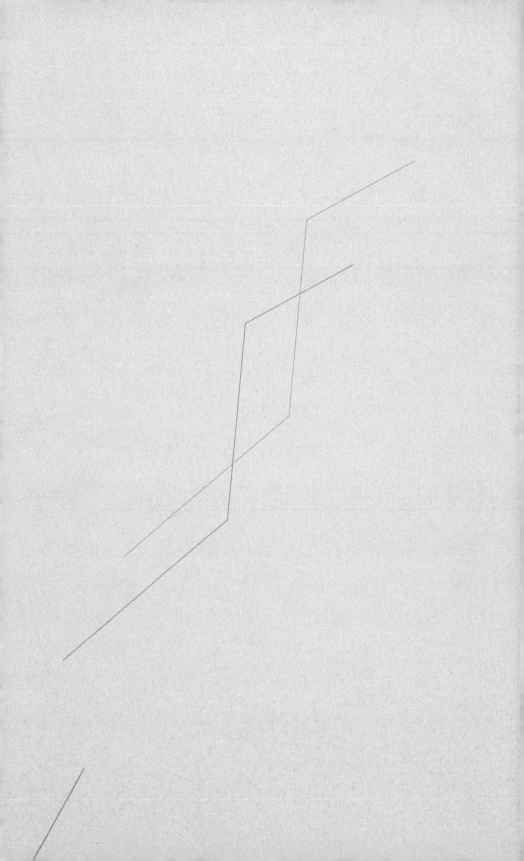

Book About a Candle Burning in a Shed

They called me down so I went down. My uniform was basically clean; a life alone makes the need for external demonstration almost disappear, but not fully. One thing I hate is when you get there and it's all over. Like felled trees after a storm you have to cut up and drag off the road. But not really the same thing. I knew it would be an important day when someone first hollered help in my direction. Mostly it is small jobs, unlocking cars and checking on the elderly. Sometimes they think I am their son and cry when I leave. Other times they are pretty much dead and I call the paramedics. None of the situations are good. I was north of town when the dispatcher crackled to me. Her clothes found in the river, hung up on some rocks, probably she got taken in the storm—but I was still uneasy, even though nature is out of my hands, which should be a relief like it is to be a child and not a man. Water's high and full of silt, and it smelled like squash bugs and my ex-girlfriend's neck when she worried about money. There was never enough of anything but I guess I got used to it. She was still beautiful from a distance and always in my memory delivered on a soft cloud. I didn't make a grab for her shirt as it drifted away, there on the banks, sun as bright as I'd ever seen it. I was afraid to be pulled under.

I missed her, but she was found later that day close to the dam. *I think there is something you ought to see*, so I went with my eyes that I might see. Hasn't been identified, but already dredged up, covered with bottom things that kids fish out with sticks. *Put a cloth over her face.* My ex-girlfriend due to marry, I heard earlier. Beside myself. River ran but I was trying not to take it personal, or the Cottonwood bent over my thinning hair, inspecting. *Come check this out,* they invited. Long scratches down her forearms, the kind you could give yourself. *What happened*, my voice from the low shrubs choking the bank. Whatever it was I don't think it started out so bad. The river looked mean, could take anyone away, especially if they weren't loved right. He came to her when I should have come to her. I tossed a rock but only got two skips. The other deputy was writing something down. Overhead, the sun a tetherball struck to the west. Kids horsing around in the park beyond. *Get home, it's darkening.* They looked at me like I could never be their father. I'm not much on games.

We have a name, I was told next morning. I'd thought of a few myself. The first white man to discover it usually stole namesake. *Who's her Daddy*, I asked. There wasn't a listing, no record sheathed in liner notes, the job of needling the song, mine. They called her C. in the reports. A good place to start a major scale, the notes would mount in time to a decent enough chorus. I wasn't yet thinking about resolve. The tremulous grass waist high at her last known address, a shed hunkered against a stand of silver birch. Where someone would go to hide if they did a bad thing or if someone had done a bad thing to them. Inside the shed were the usual materials: candle, cord of wood, sleeping bag, flashlight, some old tin cans. Hard not to judge the choice, with so many tools lying around, to not construct a plank bed at least. The single window looked out over a meadow swaying importantly. There was nothing to see but I saw it all, humming tunelessly to let anyone, anyone at all, know I was there.

The thing about being wanted for a crime is that they want you, even when they don't know who you are. I spent a lot of time thinking who I'd marry, an accompaniment to boyhood's study of the natural world, how bugs die, which side you'd take in a bar fight. The thing about being a person of interest is that they want to hear your story because they think they got it cased, and when you say it they are comforted—the way bugs die easily between palms, or a chair comes quickly over someone's head you weren't rooting for. At the local bar it didn't happen as often as we imagined, but even a good man walked in there braced. Made rounds like clockwork on night shift. It was the last place C. was seen, hair swept up, head's pedestal unadorned and skirted by a plain white t. I liked the songs they used to play, old Kitty Wells complaining about the way you were, just sitting there with your drink thinking about someone you'd best not. Someone you'd never marry. Someone you'd set on fire with a magnifying glass until her family and friends rushed out, dragging her body deep into that dirty colony you'd step all over if you could.

Thought to finger the old man reported to come out of the bushes on occasion to fill a canteen or maybe watch the children splashing on the banks like he was remembering something from back before. Never liked looking for anyone specific. If you are an ugly man it is best not to involve yourself in a particular line of searching and just be thankful for what you have. What were you doing on that particular day? *I dragged myself down to the shore thinking about a bath.* Did you bring soap? Did you bring a comb or a chamois? All negative. My girlfriend broke her leg some years ago. Had to sit on the toilet while I washed up and down her back with a sponge. Each knob of her spine I could not turn to open that little unhappy door, let it out, let it look in the mirror mouthing: *enough, already.* What is she doing on this particular day? The screen door affixed to loose hinges last I drove by. Probably the mosquitoes have no trouble entering; probably they are eating her alive, sweetest thing.

Coroner's report biblical. Sodomized, blunt force trauma. Maybe a brick from a hopeful construction site. The town dying slowly, all day I troll the someday graves thinking about flowers in her wedding bouquet—great peonies quitting on their stems, collapsing into the crook of leaves. One thing to learn is the ending. I want to go by heart attack over a snow shovel. I keep a journal of my thoughts to help in the investigation. Someone to blame: C. to be buried tomorrow. The farmers hand-mowing invasives along the perimeter are without much use for gardens that don't hock up a bundle of corn or sugar beets, so I wonder where in China her flowers are grown, which great valley laden with endings to endings. I won't ever see history for the pink face tilting heavenward. A penny and crushed aspirin in water to keep them longer.

Investigation suspended during the funeral. I attend in uniform. Most of the town came out, filled the park, heads bent, submitting to the sun. Men wore shorts. Women wore sundresses with big yellow flowers printed on them, stockings two shades too dark. I was thinking how it would feel to peel off nylons very slowly on a hot day. C. nailed into a plain wooden box. The lowering. Dense loam I tossed atop as I walked past, worms struggling to deepen themselves. I noticed my ex-girlfriend but could not determine if she was crying or sweating. No matter. No matter dark or rich enough to suffocate all of it. Afterward, people stood around clasping one another's shoulders. I kept watch for any suspicious behavior. When I heard someone laugh I touched my gun. I could not understand my loneliness, the shape of what I was looking at. My ears were full of small bells that rang for what seemed like the entire day, but was probably only a couple of hours.

Chief has a suspect. C. last seen departing the bar at 0200 with a 20-something called Isaiah (scabbard face, body the height you'd hang a deer from) then back to the only motel in town full of truckers or families too tired to care. Identifying marks on the bedclothes, nervous departure, old white Ford with a toolbox. *Go to the motel, interview the desk girl.* She was careful in exposition and full of "sir." *They were loud and full of drink sir,* her words shook out of her, turned her upside down like you do with a toaster when the bread's about to catch and the damn thing's too hot to reach for. I did not want that fire. *Please give me the keys,* and I left for the room.

Night table turned on its side, black cord with a naked bulb taped to the ceiling. Flowers all over the bedspread in a ruined garden where nary a bee would feast. The room had already been inspected, printed, proofed, I was just there to notice, to have a feeling for. I have never lain down in such a place. Woke up there some days, for sure—felt the fire ants in the throat, swallowed hotly, and just wanted to get the hell out. Yeah, I woke up in it. Sometimes she was beside me, her long yellow hair in rivulets over the pillow. I liked to brush it real slow. *What are you doing, go back to bed*, she'd instruct. But my hand was a meager skiff coursing the river of her hair—calm until I remembered the floods, the thousands of houses under water, the people that once lived in those houses, the people those people buried out back when they died from fever in the night. The fields you walk out in at dawn, mostly alone.

Back to town for provisions before calling it quits, I had to take my feelings along, but could leave 'em in the truck for an hour or so while I stocked up on what I need. They aren't going anywhere. They don't know how to drive or walk even. They cannot scatter as seed so the birds might feast, nor tap the shoulder of one I love. Motoring through the outskirts, daylight makes the downtown look like a bloated abdomen. If you are rich you live on the wings and spread out teasingly, but never have I been lifted up. Never launched into a headwind the old churches unattended, the phlegmatic bars coughing toward solvency, never carried northward are the girls leaning against the sides of buildings, their feet pointing east and west, hips thrust slightly forward the way you might push a piece of candy toward a child to distract him for a minute while you finish your thought. The child's joy upon receiving candy is not documented, and a gray torpor begins to enlace all sensual pleasure, like the duplexes with shared entryways, never decorated because they belong to no one really.

I like the photos of missing children tacked up on grocery store bulletin boards. I never remember faces so frozen, little lambs collapsed in Jesus' patient lap, mewling muffled by his great despairing cloak. *The last time you plucked lint from her blouse*, I ask myself. *The last time you made her supper or used a plastic knife to gut a fish?* I can't find my grocery list, the objective of my starved meanderings. Each face throws off a dim light. I recognize the outlines, their tracks in imagined hoarfrost, the way they might have said *excuse me* in these aisles of mass replication, the new oppression of choice. I draw a picture of what I ate for dinner the night she disappeared. *If you have information on the whereabouts* . . . no. I draw a picture of what I will eat for dinner next year. It looks the same only I am older; my hand trained on the detail of gravy, a thick reduction smothers each thing I imagine. I draw a picture of the grocery store. If it burns down, I will tack it up in another grocery store. *If you have any information please contact.* I'm trying to focus on the distinctive way the carts are strewn over the parking lot, a plastic bag aloft over rows of old trucks, the beautiful woman, dark hair across her face, starting a van.

Tuesday meeting: Chief reports there's evidence Isaiah fled to Canada. I laugh at what's not funny, dispersion from one threat to another, the migration of birds, how far you can get on a tank of gas. Never paid much mind to where a man comes from. Mother was a bathrobe over the couch, though I rarely steady myself on a chair and just take in night air, damn crickets making love, people too, without meaning much more than what loading docks do, fill up with stuff you might use for a few months then ignore. See? Couldn't pay it much mind. Best friend as a boy got to college on his mother's love, though he wasn't any smarter than the rest, his boots always used or a knock-off brand sagging laceless around the ankles. Never played god to another, sure did help some, but elevation always happened to the side of where I stood, the grass climbing to the sky, or him 15 years past pulling out of his carport, smiling to himself. Mostly I observe deep frowns behind the wheel and none of us got more than an hour away but this one guy. Should check in with him. My ex wanted work at the dentist's office. *You'll get sick from it.* I was thinking about where those mouths had been, my mother's final reeking words, the way the chief told us it's international, the Feds are coming in. I wanted to be something else, the kind of thing that needed tending. New model pickup an old friend washed every Sunday afternoon, by hand, then drove far away.

Called out during the meeting to break up a fight down County Line Road. On my way found a young girl, too young to be walking so alone. *I'll get you an ice cream* from the half-rolled window. She came inside shyly, the air-con blew her skin to clumsy pointillism, though she'd never look put-together, even from afar. *Where you headed*, trying to be casual with the youth. I don't want their trouble. *To the river*, she never looked at me directly, ate quickly. I observed the serious way she wiped her mouth with the napkin as a sort of self-discipline. *I bet you're plenty smart.* She let herself out in front of the drugstore, did not thank me. My girlfriend wanted two of them, a boy and a girl, said the world was good enough to my precluding gloom. *But is there more?* What did I mean. Where did it live outside of me, freely, where was my finger pointing, *like this*. **This** beautiful sunset in our bills. **These** holy intimations of budding trees, our drive to work. When I got to County Line, the fight was over, some guys were baling hay and laughing. *What took you so long?*

Feds throughout the office like a fence tumbled down. Felt sorry for Chief, their pity for his age, simple straight talk—he still champs protocol and knows how to help foal a horse crying out and stuck in the push. *Put your hands right up there*, he'd say to a bewildered stableman, and they always did it fairly. The Feds didn't know. Would have cut a mare open, *at least we saved one*, I can hear them congratulate. I've only handled a few horses. There're great trails just out of town, but you have to be careful of roots and holes that curry a stumble, the horse with a broken leg who can't be limped home. Officially off the case, I worry C's trail is not being visited. In town, no mention of her name, mothers no longer pulling their children in tightly at the sight of a stranger, the memorial by the banks blown into the river. Every night I clean my ears, brush my teeth, say my girlfriend's name at the mirror. Her name starts out real low and rises to an *ee*, so that my mouth pulls back as if by bit. My head yanks away from the sink but I don't know where to run for her and if I let myself think about it, won't sleep.

Off the case does not forsake a man completely. Went back to C.'s shed for more research and to destroy any pictures I happened across. Stub of a candle burning brightly, illuminating not much beyond arm's reach. Found nothing more incriminating than evidence some kids had been meddling, maybe having at each other like animals in the dark, and a book about a woman working in the mills many miles from here that I thumbed through until my eyes gave me trouble. Her name was Emmeline. She died in a hard winter and there was a scandal that I didn't work to find in the text but could feel all around it. Left quickly for the barracks, the drive I don't recall. A little later: Chief, I want to tell you something. *Why are you getting your mind wrapped like a car around a tree?* I was aware of being remembered this way: jotting down notes on the accident's prim sideline, gore untethered to my right, my inevitable headstone etched with "I observed." No, I said. The town is in danger. The town bludgeoned by a dense unawareness, as when my girlfriend waited until the lights were dimmed to unbutton her blouse. To come blindly to a thing so beautiful. To turn away as if not seeing was a choice.

5:30 am, thinking. No one's interested in sacrifice as a construct and I'm not either. Mad about her death, about her leaving for another life. They are closer every day to extradition, and I wonder after last supper, when all is said and done. We don't want the mercy of fried chicken and cold pilsner and pie. I'd eat hard tack with lard for time immortal given the real chance to say my piece: Crime I don't know more. Isaiah's no different I assume. Chief tells he's fathered a minor's unborn. She's wayward up north, a local girl looking out at the wrong horizon, all full up and humming with his refrain. A life of jingles I try to squeeze out to quiet the mind. Hush, hush at the breast where we all were, once. There is your mother. There's the sun, straddling you, her hair sweeping across your eyes. There's your clothes in a pile on the linoleum, which is also yours, which shines for only you. I don't mention the dreams: Roadkill coming back to life, the answers I don't have but am asked for by an angry mob. What we do with details is not unlike touching a thing that doesn't want to be touched, a thing that would wheel around and bite the hand if only it could. The part of hunger we deserve.

All the way to the barracks a cold crosswind through the pickup. To which great monument has the finitude of this morning been pointing? I hear from myself the end's *kerplonk*: the roadside daisies coughing dust in my wake, every door I had the nerve to close slamming in unison. What retrospective have I compiled, notes cribbed depicting such cold descent? I begin: I knew a dead girl, clothes dropped to the ground as commanded by the equator's dependable warmth. Then lower through the mountains the script went, getting colder, you are getting colder, you are freezing by the second page of notes. It's a game I used to play with my girlfriend. Mostly she wanted me to bring her something from her purse slung over the chair, but I liked to drag it out, on hands and knees looking under the bed or feeling along her dresses lined up in the closet. No, get up and turn left. Now you're warmer. I walked around behind her, loose strands curling around her ponytail I liked to roll between my fingers. You're so hot you are burning up. I stepped back, way too far. You're cold again. Her delicate finger pointing to the hall that touched me some nights until I shivered. You're so far away. You're an iceberg in the ocean and you will melt and be forgotten.

A celebratory mood transfixes a man but his problems still dangle intact like crude words in a pleasure church. Isaiah's nabbed and the posse's gesturing to one another freely, tossing cans around the office, knowing that if they were a pack in the wild, they wouldn't be hungry for a few days and could chill with the bitches and maybe watch their pup tumble out of a den and look upon the world with wonder. Last night the Feds rolled in off a tip, 20 miles past the border, nothing but pines in steadfast community pushing in toward town. No struggle, no plea—let himself into the back of the van like he was heading to the market. The posse knows what it would have done differently: run. *I'd rather be shot informally in the back. I'd rather the sword drawn in a blink than the slow soul ransack led by the State.* I don't believe them. They'd want the treatment. Try coming home to the note: I've gone for good. Let's hit the bars. They're whistling. A toast to C. To the memory of C. To the memory of the memory of C., before there were gardens, the water-treatment facility, a woman sleeping in a covered wagon, nightgown twisted around her waist, waking up somewhere new, *don't be afraid, I will protect you*, before law. The drink brings afternoon burn to the eye of a patron. *Good job*, says he don't have one himself. I write his name on a scrap of paper, tuck it into my pocket. *There is no such thing as safekeeping*, I say. He nods.

It goes on like this and suddenly Saturday. Regarding the bar processional: they come in their best and leave in pairs baptizing with the mouth or a laying on of hands to steady a shake in the thigh. The posse strewn from darts to dance floor, I too am a disciple of collect and scatter, with the birds around a shake of seed, then alone in the tree to watch for danger. Nothing to eat away the wooze, I perch. A girl walks into the bar. Have you heard this one before? A girl walks into a bar: I'll have what he's having. And she has his face. A girl walks into a bar, I'll take a two-fister. She grabs his hands and yanks. A girl walks into the bar: Help me get my daddy home, and I'm out of the trees. We get him as far as North Ave. and he's sick in the street. Do I have to clean up the mess she wants to know. Naw, the rain'll right it, though the storm has seemingly passed. She has her arms folded across her chest and her face is a narrow scratch-plough over my body. I step into the shadow, I walk away from the light, where the dirt of me cannot be turned over, cannot be dug into. *You can take it from here.*

Everything closed up, awnings rolled back, the neon sign from the bar washes the sidewalk in boreal pink. I touch the door to push in but with my second thought move past. My ex's house round the corner dimmed but for a single light in the kitchen like the candle burning in C.'s small shed. I went inside once when no one was home just to make sure and maybe press her coat collar to my face. I can hear music from the backroom, the kind to keep you company if sleep is what you're after and like most cannot enact your desire. I peer into the window and see only a reflection of myself peering into the window. I'm working on the case of where it all went wrong, when I hear my radio crackle and splinter. It's full of old bones: Some John Doe in the park with a 6-pack. Another John Doe doing a buck twenty on County Line Road. The detail that he is alone allows me to ignore the call. Hours pass, and what becomes clear is that she is dreaming. I add the word *alone* to my case notes for when I'm interviewed by the State. The word covers the page like a river, a river that moves a body toward its banks, a river that isn't cruel or hopeful as it runs past town toward the ocean, never turning back.

The State has its case. The State wants to sleep easily, through the strung-out cries of its young, through the shuttering of the mill and the men and women fighting deep into the night over who gets to use the car in the morning. I focus on the facts as they stand, but the State wants them prone, wants them on the floor, covered in blood. This is how things are built: No one is loved, no one is saved. I write a victim impact statement the way I'd want to hear it. It starts with an image of horses leaping from a burning barn. Sorrysorrysorry the world has a big slash in it, and if you think the wound is sexy or helpful, at the end of the statement I will set fire to the abutting pasture, too. The State calls another, then another, until it hears the shape of its bed. The State turns to face the wall. The State closes its eyes, relaxes its jaw. The State rests.

LOVE POEM #41

The width of the word no,
to live in its shelter
without the precious ones you love

your love, a raccoon ripping
through the screen door—
garbage strewn about.

ELLESMERE ISLAND

You have a job at a pet store. $12/hour. You face the leashes and dog toys, clean the cages and place the rodents destined for the boa constrictor into the freezer first, because you've read Jack London and know that they will go numb, which will hurt, but then they will go to sleep, which is, in your experience, gentle. There is a heroin epidemic in your small, northern town. People going numb all over the place. You don't know their names, you don't name them. Lake Hazen, on Ellesmere Island, is a thermal oasis. In the summer it gets so warm you can walk in up to your neck. Still, everyone craves the buried heart 1,000 meters deep in the ice. It'll take a bomb to open that baby up, to expose those guts, to get to the thing we all take for granted as alive. You're comforted by Ellesmere Island, where rats might sleep for thousands of years, waiting for scientists to chip them out, to insert the long needle into their necks. A man rushes in, holds up the pet store with a fishing knife. For a moment you are frozen, but then you put the bills on the counter and raise your hands in the air. The beast in the freezer shifts on the rack, closes its eyes. The man does the same in the parking lot. 120 people visit Lake Hazen every summer and post pictures. During your lunch break you scroll through them on your phone.

SPRINGTIME IN AMERICA

Wonder of the tires burning across the lake
I am burning—they are no longer necessary
to this great plan for living right.

Wonder I once drank the water—fronds of bracken,
all, from the mouth to the belly. Whatever he says,
the deeper his touch.

Will I ever get the answer—wonder of the road
that leads somewhere pleasant. A picnic table
at the edge of a storming lake, was this
to mean I would be safe if I could see danger—

He was so beautiful, above and below. The cavern
of his hands, leaves across my face—
his wooden back a dock. I lie there, wait for sun.

Men continue to work so they might continue
to work—weekends, the only time to rest
on a shore of tangleberry and hacklebush—
sleep through the twigs scribbling over soft flesh.

I was asleep through the scratching, still,
I heard the dogs. You know those dogs?
I heard the shape of their need like black plastic ballooning
over the garden bed, like men and their whistles trilling.

Wonder of the rising up. Three days, fifty days—
what could I do but rinse off, stuff an iris in my ear—?

He was so beautiful, above—flocks of hunger,
below—roots of hunger. Born knowing how
to survive by making a simple sound or two—I asked
for a single buttercup. I was given a field to manage.

How the Town Looks

Trash brought to the side of the road.
Don't know who bothered. Bucket loader

gathers snow in its cradle, mounds it
in the park next to the hospital.

Forceps take the head and pull, metal seeks flesh,
seeks to trifle and injure. Mother who gave you can

take you away; cry out in floodlit hallway.
Animated husks, faces of softening putty,

faces of braided twigs, every single one
of them loved at least once.

Pasture of small withers. Do-it-this-way schoolyard.
They will ask you to remove the clothes, they will provide

a uniform, money with rent already taken out.
Sex to make someone feel better, sex

so you don't have to listen, sex in the room
where the TV spills blue light all over

bodies, like galaxies, there isn't space
for more than one on the same path.

Someone gets lost. Someone shoots a noisy dog.
Guttered leaves are dumped into bags.

They are simple words: limp, wet, cold.
They are easy to dispose. Rusted dumpster

next to the library. A car screeching down Main.
How the town looks. How we treat the mentally ill.

MADE TO LIE DOWN IN GREEN PASTURES

To admire the idea of sponsorship.
To fail intimately, reduce that
which was counted on. The President
called us to the pasture, fie on us—!
the factory of larkspur, nettle mouth,
withered stamen, daisy, daisy blade.

To which ruminant woman the burden
of birth endured? I was asked
by my President to lie down.
I love my country, the magnitude of its longing
precluded by a tendency to give up, throw down

walk away from the pasture to the edge
of a nascent wood—silver
and encroaching—so youthful is that
which moves forward ho! I love my country,

the blank middle brain of it, fulvous
and waving at anyone who happens by.
The salt lake lick, the mountainous tumult
hewn to shale dagger and feldspar
knit to some idea of rising up. In spite
of erosion, my President begged:

lie down in the green pasture and I did
not question, I love my country, I did.

Sponsorship was the way he gave me time.
My President was fettered, busy nobilizing
grass and sheep, inculcating the bellwether,
nursing tiller and stolon,
hitched to every breath and sound
in the kingdom, the specific need of wheat, for wheat,
exhausted by multiplication, welcoming
each tremulous seed blown from each pod.

I did not expect to be noticed. You might say
I hungered to be noticed, but kept from myself
that black freckle on this otherwise pale plain,
the place on the body one touches alone
and unconsciously, lying in the pasture, just lying
all of the time as my President requested.

His sponsorship included a kitchen table—
cherry with a cross-hatched inlay and delicate
folding legs. Sitting there one had the perfect view
of the quiet brook, and if that's your scene
you can sit there forever,
unnoticed and mossing up.

I will show you how to get here,
my President promised, but I
was all up inside a taxicab or a plane
circling the pasture. A woman stretches her arm
out the window bestride the violence
of wind. I am the woman with violence
all over her face and arms
but that doesn't mean I cannot lie still.

Gentle stable, hayed floor,
sidled-up-to-body—never the mind,
not even searching for that needle,
I was made to lie down.

I used to line up all of the beer cans
in tidy rows along the stonewall.
I did this because I wanted attention.
I know you are thinking of that pun about
dead soldiers; I know you are praying
for someone to come back to you.
My President spreads his elegant hands over
the lectern, his voice contains the grain
of raw bacon, you can feel him separating
in strips. He holds his breath,
closes his eyes to the pasture.
I stand at attention.

Sometimes my country is a dark vale
over which my President looms,
portentous, struggling at the border.
I once loved a man by covering my face
with the sheets and not peeking.
I once loved a man by pretending the sea
was his mouth. I walked in up to my waist.
I once loved a man by dwindling—
an ordinary stone skipped into a river.
The water runs over and over. I am still
at the bottom of that one.

My President restored the faith I had in pairs:
I shall walk beside another of my own making.
In another time there was a boat tossed in the swell
like a furious exchange, like he hated me and the stall
we occupied together, when you are the smaller one,
kicking his rib: *take her by the left leg*
and throw her down the stairs.

Our small apartment faced the park.
My President sent his very best.
I wore the barren ice-field dress
until the grass began to poke through.
One morning I woke up alone—
I could hear only the clock's rigid insistence:
How many more hours until you join
the pasture. I wandered.

Have you seen a country in retreat?
The smiling Florida coast palmed and beat at.
The dumbed-over steel mills cursing the capital
just far enough away not to get punched.
I took cover in a job for 8 years
too good for anything that is finite
love or the pasture, could not be led.

No, no. I was made to lie.
The pasture: Kelly, pine, seafoam
mantis, tea and hooker. My President
was specific and I was a description
of Nebraska, moved through forever

like a game of monopoly or a job.
At a certain point you lose focus
and then you are in Colorado:

Men with black labs wearing
bandannas in the back of pickups.
Women with bicycles and yoga
and hair you run through and beer
the flavor of Christmas trees.
If I work sixty hours I can finally
have something good.
This sounds funny,
but never was I so afraid.

I had to risk everything to lie.
Against my back the soil. Against
my back the long blades.
Against my back the poor, their needs,
the one I love, blocking the light
in the shape of a man. I looked
up at the sky and thought I saw the majesty,
a clerk-cum-CEO, the path beat
by a plane going somewhere—
the violence of going going gone—
the violence of standing at the edge
of a park kicking a stone, couples stretched
out on blankets as far as the eye can see.

40 years stuck in this form,
never pretty enough to cut in line.

The President asked, *please wait your turn.*
But who can be patient, Mister President,
for the quiet waters?

So I circled the defensive wall,
the outworks and the earthworks—
dolefully a rampart stands, but how does she lie?
I told him I could see, I told him I would stay awake
until dawn and when it came my President glared at me
proud, red, the Denver skyline winked in the distance,
a broken field tilled before frost.

Quit the job for your own name's sake.
You hail from cattails in twilight
valorous and cascading over the pond.
From the eyes of potatoes blinking in the shed.
You hail from beating through new growth—
suckling trees, sissy birds, animal paths that Waterloo.

From a parking lot puddle that contained
a rainbow, the rich smell of the nozzle
pulled from the gas can—
from streamers in front of used car lots,
the boy wearing a mattress costume
ushering you into a mattress store
and where he will go when his summer job ends.

So I walked until I reached a barn
6 months, 9 months, you get the idea.
I came upon it and pressed my back to its door
as a bulwark I leaned in until the door fell
away and I was all that was left.

I let the animals out of their stalls,
whispered *you are free* as I lay in the pasture.
Awaited the trample, the stampede—
to be covered by their freedom,
the sharp edge of their release
digging into my soft belly,
grinding me down in the grass,
to which my President might entreat:
Run for your life!

I cannot say how long I remained,
but they never came out to join me.
Babies were born, babies were born
babies were born again and again.
Is there nothing so extraordinary as
the tirade of successors willing to lie?

The pasture became a lonely cornfield
and I, its faithful ear, could hear
only from afar the braying and lowing,
the purring and pecking and squawking,
growling, howling, mewling and snorting.

Like those adolescent nights, alone in your bedroom
when you cried out but did not know for whom,
or that your cry would grow limbs, tower over a basin,
splash its face with cold water. Get up!
Go forth and meet it on any corner! Grab it
by the collar and never let it go!

Exposure

He looked better on the internet, broken up in outer space, reassembled next to their smiling dog on a flatscreen. A walker came each day, ran the dog through the small park across from the home they used to share. Still, she dreamt the dog bounding over drifts, scrambling across soft ice, dew claws cut up from the effort to reach a distant fire or motel lobby. He looked better in the polaroid shook by its edges over the parking lot, the dog a blur behind him. It wanted to run forever but he could not abide the longing of others. The wind was a smear of cold cream after curtain call; the moonlight was serviceable. He looked better in still-life, the canvas unprepped so the cloth bore its weave across his face. Someone made this man over and over. She dreamt him matches and kindling, a couple of flares, a handsome coat, someone to call out to. He called her baby after sex, like he had made her. She did not dream this. He looked better in photographs, developed in the dark, like some deep-eyed potato minding the root cellar. Someone who can see the shadow, but keeps it to himself. In minus 10°F women and men suffer differently—women are more likely to develop disfiguring frostbite, while men remain intact until they die. The women survive; they can take it, the ugliness. Dogs come back, lie atop them. Dogs come back with hatchets and flashlights. Do not judge what must be done to survive. What must be cleaned up after. She knew nothing of exposure—had only dreamt him gone from her in one quick and blinding flash, enough for the dog to see its way back. And when the dog finally returned, it often licked the air around her hands where her fingers used to be.

TRESTLE

Could not give up the men
by burning. The cock by final stroke.
The cock by axe blow. Baseball.
Rid not the dry goods by mouth
or bottled water, uncapped.

Did not the dress by taking off,
nor the flower by plucking
the field clean.
Girls by their own two hands,
not with a winch or a book.

Would not the hand by gripping tight,
the flailing one by shepherd's crook.
The danger was in the distance between,
not the grace of the reach.

Listen. Not by the sea with its droll
slap. Not with a fussy cap pulled low.
The lazy grief of the harbor.

Let me see your eyes. No, your real ones:
The overgrown trestle above the dam.
How it feels to leap.

THE LAST THING YOU SEE

It's not the last thing you see
pulling out of the driveway—

weeds urging the gravel to recede.
A growing over of dimming light.

Goodbye nestled-in spoon.
The tray's infinite holding. Goodbye

what was lifted to the mouth—a pasture
beyond. Ruminants milling the green blades.

It's not the thing you wanted
a piece of : the way it would feel

in a different life. A hand on the small of the back
urging you forward. The way it would feel.

Later, neighbor judgment.
See you, apron accusing.

The ones you love incompletely
the ones you love and suffer—
sheets kicked to the bed's sloped edge.

The way it would look—
can you tell me how it looks?

Where it was last seen? Can you
tell me what color the hair and the eyes?

It's not the last thing you see
pulling out of the driveway.

It looks like I wished I had loved
more. The moon was enough

of a dress. It ran through the woods
is how it felt.

Goodbye cupboard rifle. Put
the dog out. The sound of a train

in the distance never really motivated
anything, unless you count the grass—

unless you count the grass lying down at its side.

What is that number precisely? Can you
count it on your hands?

It's not the last thing you see
pulling out of the driveway.

The stars multiplied in the rearview
mirror. The stars that could be dead

flicked over the night sky. They were inviting,
like clear ponds where cattle gather.

I was so thirsty, I had to turn around.

NOTES

Book About a Candle Burning in a Shed: *A life alone makes the need for external demonstration disappear* is taken from Admiral Richard E. Byrd's remarkable memoir, *Alone*.

ACKNOWLEDGMENTS

Gratitude to the editors of *Coppernickel*, *Pinwheel*, above/ground press, and *Roads Taken: Contemporary Vermont Poetry*, where poems from this book have appeared, sometimes in different versions.

Always appreciating DJ Dolack, Christopher Kiely, Saskia Kiely, Tinder Kiely, Elizabeth Ready, Michael Robbins, and Allison Titus, for their care of me and my work. Thanks also to Paul Slovak and the Boomerang Foundation for their support.

Paige Ackerson-Kiely is the author of two poetry
collections, *In No One's Land* and *My Love Is a
Dead Arctic Explorer*. She is a generalist and lives in
Peekskill, New York.

JOHN ASHBERY
Selected Poems
Self-Portrait in a Convex
Mirror

PAIGE ACKERSON-KIELY
Dolefully, A Rampart
Stands

PAUL BEATTY
Joker, Joker, Deuce

JOSHUA BENNETT
The Sobbing School

TED BERRIGAN
The Sonnets

LAUREN BERRY
The Lifting Dress

PHILIP BOOTH
Lifelines: Selected Poems
1950–1999

JULIANNE BUCHSBAUM
The Apothecary's Heir

JIM CARROLL
Fear of Dreaming: The
Selected Poems
Living at the Movies
Void of Course

ALISON HAWTHORNE DEMING
Genius Loci
Rope
Stairway to Heaven

CARL DENNIS
Another Reason
Callings
New and Selected Poems
1974–2004
Night School
Practical Gods
Ranking the Wishes
Unknown Friends

DIANE DI PRIMA
Loba

STUART DISCHELL
Dig Safe

STEPHEN DOBYNS
Velocities: New and
Selected Poems:
1966–1992

EDWARD DORN
Way More West

ROGER FANNING
The Middle Ages

ADAM FOULDS
The Broken Word

CARRIE FOUNTAIN
Burn Lake
Instant Winner

AMY GERSTLER
Crown of Weeds
Dearest Creature
Ghost Girl
Medicine
Nerve Storm
Scattered at Sea

EUGENE GLORIA
Drivers at the Short-Time
Motel
Hoodlum Birds
My Favorite Warlord

DEBORA GREGER
By Herself
Desert Fathers, Uranium
Daughters
God
In Darwin's Room
Men, Women, and Ghosts
Western Art

TERRANCE HAYES
American Sonnets for
My Past and Future
Assassin
Hip Logic
How to Be Drawn
Lighthead
Wind in a Box

NATHAN HOKS
The Narrow Circle

ROBERT HUNTER
Sentinel and Other Poems

MARY KARR
Viper Rum

JACK KEROUAC
Book of Blues
Book of Haikus
Book of Sketches

JOANNA KLINK
Circadian
Excerpts from a Secret
Prophecy
Raptus

JOANNE KYGER
As Ever: Selected Poems

ANN LAUTERBACH
Hum
If in Time: Selected Poems,
1975–2000
On a Stair
Or to Begin Again
Spell
Under the Sign

CORINNE LEE
Plenty

PHILLIS LEVIN
May Day
Mercury
Mr. Memory & Other
Poems

PATRICIA LOCKWOOD
Motherland Fatherland
Homelandsexuals

WILLIAM LOGAN
Macbeth in Venice
Madame X
Rift of Light
Strange Flesh
The Whispering Gallery

J. MICHAEL MARTINEZ
Museum of the Americas

ADRIAN MATEJKA
The Big Smoke
Map to the Stars
Mixology

MICHAEL MCCLURE
Huge Dreams: San
Francisco and Beat
Poems

ROSE MCLARNEY
Its Day Being Gone

DAVID MELTZER
David's Copy: The Selected
Poems of David Meltzer

ROBERT MORGAN
Dark Energy
Terroir

CAROL MUSKE-DUKES
Blue Rose
An Octave Above Thunder
Red Trousseau
Twin Cities

ALICE NOTLEY
Certain Magical Acts
Culture of One
The Descent of Alette
Disobedience
In the Pines
Mysteries of Small Houses

WILLIE PERDOMO
The Crazy Bunch
The Essential Hits of
Shorty Bon Bon

LIA PURPURA
It Shouldn't Have Been
Beautiful

LAWRENCE RAAB
The History of Forgetting
Visible Signs: New and
Selected Poems

BARBARA RAS
The Last Skin
One Hidden Stuff

MICHAEL ROBBINS
Alien vs. Predator
The Second Sex

PATTIANN ROGERS
Generations
Holy Heathen Rhapsody
Quickening Fields
Wayfare

SAM SAX
Madness

ROBYN SCHIFF
A Woman of Property

WILLIAM STOBB
Absentia
Nervous Systems

TRYFON TOLIDES
An Almost Pure Empty
Walking

SARAH VAP
Viability

ANNE WALDMAN
Gossamurmur
Kill or Cure
Manatee/Humanity
Structure of the World
Compared to a Bubble
Trickster Feminism

JAMES WELCH
Riding the Earthboy 40

PHILIP WHALEN
Overtime: Selected Poems

ROBERT WRIGLEY
Anatomy of Melancholy
and Other Poems
Beautiful Country
Box
Earthly Meditations: New
and Selected Poems
Lives of the Animals
Reign of Snakes

MARK YAKICH
The Importance of Peeling
Potatoes in Ukraine
Unrelated Individuals
Forming a Group
Waiting to Cross